ADJECTIVES IN ORDER

Put the adjectives in the correct order in the sentences.
Write the new sentence on the line.

Hint: Adjectives should go in order starting with quantity, then value, then size, then color, and finally, material.

1. The villager wore a **robe**. (white, long)

_____.

2. I am building a **shelter**. (big, cobblestone, gray)

_____.

3. An **apple** cured the zombie villager. (golden, rare, single)

_____.

4. Watch out for the **Ender** dragon! (dangerous, black)

_____.

5. The Nether is full of **resources**. (valuable, many)

_____.

SENTENCES

A **sentence** is a group of words that tells a complete thought. All sentences begin with a **capital letter**. A statement ends with a **period**. A sentence includes a **noun**, a **verb**, and sometimes an **adjective** or **adverb**.

ADVERB describes a verb, sometimes ends in "ly"

VERB an action word, like *run*

ADJECTIVE a describing word, like *scary*

NOUN a person, place or thing, like *creeper*

Read the sentences on the opposite page and follow the instructions below.

- Draw a triangle around the **capital letter** that begins the sentence.

- Circle the **noun** (there may be more than one).

- Underline the **verb**.

- Draw a rectangle around the **adjective** and **adverbs**.

- Draw a square around the **period** that ends the sentence.

WRITING FOR MINECRAFTERS

Grade 4

Sky Pony Press
New York

Copyright © 2019 by Hollan Publishing, Inc.

Minecraft® is a registered trademark of Notch Development AB.

The Minecraft game is copyright © Mojang AB.

All rights reserved. No part of this book may be reproduced in any manner without the express written consent of the publisher, except in the case of brief excerpts in critical reviews or articles. All inquiries should be addressed to Sky Pony Press, 307 West 36th Street, 11th Floor, New York, NY 10018.

Sky Pony Press books may be purchased in bulk at special discounts for sales promotion, corporate gifts, fund-raising, or educational purposes. Special editions can also be created to specifications. For details, contact the Special Sales Department, Sky Pony Press, 307 West 36th Street, 11th Floor, New York, NY 10018 or info@skyhorsepublishing.com.

Sky Pony® is a registered trademark of Skyhorse Publishing, Inc.®, a Delaware corporation.

Visit our website at www.skyponypress.com.

10 9 8 7 6 5 4 3 2 1

Library of Congress Cataloging-in-Publication Data is available on file.

Cover design by Brian Peterson
Cover illustration by Bill Greenhead

Interior illustrations by Amanda Brack
Book design by Kevin Baier

Print ISBN: 978-1-5107-4121-8

Printed in China

A NOTE TO PARENTS

When you want to reinforce classroom skills at home, it's crucial to have kid-friendly learning materials. This *Writing for Minecrafters* workbook transforms writing practice into an irresistible adventure complete with diamond swords, zombies, skeletons, and creepers. That means less arguing over homework and more fun overall.

Writing for Minecrafters is also fully aligned with National Common Core Standards for 4th-grade writing. What does that mean, exactly? All of the writing skills taught in this book correspond to what your child is expected to learn in school. This eliminates confusion and builds confidence for greater homework-time success!

Whether it's the joy of seeing their favorite game characters on every page or the thrill of writing about Steve and Alex, there is something in this workbook to entice even the most reluctant writer.

Happy adventuring!

SENSORY DETAIL

Use lots of detail to make your writing more interesting and fun to read. Finish the sentences below with sensory detail. You'll need to first imagine what each item feels, tastes, looks, sounds, or smells like.

1. The zombie sounded _____

_____.

2. She grabbed the Ender pearl, and it felt _____

_____ in her hand.

3. The pufferfish tasted _____.

4. Up close, the portal looked _____

_____.

5. The sound the pickaxe made as it hit the redstone ore was

_____.

1. 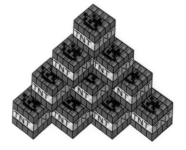 The scary wither angrily attacks a player.

2.  A dizzy zombie groans loudly.

3. A skeleton secretly fires poison arrows.

4.  Quickly hide your loot in a large chest.

5.  Never approach an exploding creeper.

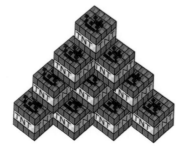

REDSTONE RESEARCH

There are lots of uses for redstone in Minecraft. Do you know them all? With an adult's help, do some online research to learn a few new ways to use redstone. List those ways below.

1. _____

_____

2. _____

_____

3. _____

_____

4. _____

_____

HEADINGS FOR HEROES

Read the paragraph and give it a heading that describes what the paragraph is about. Write it on the line provided.

HEADING: _____

There are many different weapons that players can use to battle mobs in Minecraft. You can craft a bow and arrow, an axe, or a sword if you have the right resources. Each weapon has a different benefit. Axes deal a lot of damage with each blow, but swords are best for most battles because they deliver quick hits in rapid sequence. When you play Minecraft, you learn about weapons very quickly.

HEADING: _____

Minecraft was first released in 2009. There was nothing else like it, so people immediately liked it. It was invented by a Swedish man named Markus Perrson. The earliest form of the game was very simple. Sand, lava, and water were some of the original features. Creepers were the first mob to appear in the game's Survival Mode.

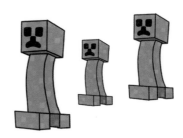

QUOTATION MARKS

A ghast has stolen all the quotation marks from the paragraph below. To defeat the ghast, add the quotation marks where they belong.

Alex was getting tired of fighting Creeper. She put down her sword. Steve is having a party, she said. Want to come?

Creeper looked confused. What is a party? he asked.

It's a lot of fun. Come and I'll show you.

When they arrived at Steve's house, Creeper saw kids running in the backyard and streamers and balloons hanging from the ceiling. A table was piled with presents, cupcakes, and party hats.

Hi, Alex. Thanks for coming to my party, Steve said.

Happy birthday, Steve, Alex replied. This is Creeper.

Creeper looked frightened. Steve handed him a piece of cake on a plate with a fork. Creeper didn't know what the fork was for, so he used his feet to eat. It's delicious, he said with his mouth full.

FACT VS. OPINION

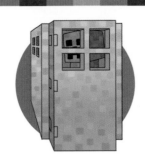

*A **fact** is something that can be proven true. An **opinion** is your personal feeling about a topic, or your point of view. Read each sentence below, and then decide whether it is a fact or an opinion. Write "F" for fact or "O" for opinion on the line.*

_____ **1.** Minecraft is a very difficult game to play.

_____ **2.** Minecraft is best played in Creative Mode.

_____ **3.** Exploding creepers can damage a player.

_____ **4.** Pigs can be tamed with a carrot.

_____ **5.** The Enderman is the scariest of all the mobs.

_____ **6.** You need 24 blocks of diamonds to make a

full suit of armor.

PLAN YOUR WRITING

Which of the following tools is the best one to have in Minecraft? Choose one and list your ideas below. Then write your paragraph on the next page.

My choice: _____

Reason #1 for my choice: _____

    Fact or detail for reason #1: _____

    Fact or detail for reason #1: _____

Reason #2 for my choice: _____

    Fact or detail for reason #2: _____

    Fact or detail for reason #2: _____

Conclusion: _____

_____

WRITE YOUR OPINION

Using the outline, or plan, you made on the previous page, write a complete paragraph. First you will state your point of view and then give two reasons why it's true. Provide two facts or details that support each reason. Finally, write your conclusion.

In my opinion, the best tool to have in Minecraft is _____

_____

_____

_____

_____

_____

_____

_____

_____

_____

COMMONLY CONFUSED WORDS

Some words sound the same but are spelled differently.
Choose the correct word from the box to complete the sentence.
Some words may be used more than once.

their	they're	there

1. Alex and Steve laugh at _____ joke.

2. The brewing stand is over _____ .

3. The witches will use eye of Ender in _____ potion.

4. Even when zombies travel in a mob, _____ very slow.

its	it's

5. The arctic fox blends in well with _____ surroundings.

6. _____ important to water your crops every day.

7. When TNT explodes, _____ noisy.

to	two	too

8. The _____ creepers are dancing.

9. The health meter can never be _____ full.

10. The iron golem hands a poppy _____ the villager.

11. You need _____ tripwire hooks _____ make a tripwire trap.

loose	lose

12. The animals have gotten _____ from their pen.

13. Make a compass so you do not _____ your way in Minecraft.

WRITE ABOUT A TOPIC

*Which is your favorite way to play Minecraft, in Survival, Creative, Adventure, Spectator, or Hardcore mode? Explain why. Be sure to include **definitions** for tricky words that readers might not know. Add plenty of **details** to support your ideas.*

_____

_____

_____

_____

_____

_____

_____

_____

_____

_____

_____

LINKING IDEAS IN YOUR WRITING

*To group types of information together, use **linking words**. Some examples of linking words are:* another, **for example**, **also**, **next**, *and* **because**. *Revise the paragraph you wrote on the previous page adding linking words.*

_____

_____

_____

_____

_____

_____

_____

_____

_____

_____

RELATIVE PRONOUNS

*A **relative pronoun** refers back to a noun that was already mentioned. Some examples of relative pronouns are: **that**, **which**, **who**, **whose**, and **whom**. Circle the relative pronoun in the sentences below.*

1. Minecraft is the video game that most kids play.

2. Minecraft, which can be played in Survival Mode or

Creative Mode, is exciting.

3. Pigs are animals that can be tamed with a carrot.

4. Is that the mob that chased you?

5. The Enderman that finishes first wins the race.

6. The player who built the snow golem is very clever.

7. That's the chest which holds her armor.

8. That's the player whose armor is gold.

MORE RELATIVE PRONOUNS

Fill in the blank with a word from the box. Who and whose refer to people. That refers to things. Underline the person or thing that the relative pronoun refers to. The first one is done for you.

who	whose	that

1. Alex is the <u>girl</u> _____who_____ is hugging the pig.

2. The diamond _____ Alex is holding is shiny.

3. The diamond sword _____ Steve made is very sharp.

4. The witch _____ potion I used is wearing a purple robe.

5. The villager _____ grew the glistening melon is a good farmer.

PRESENT PROGRESSIVE TENSE

Progressive verb tenses are used to talk about an action that is in progress. This can be something that is happening now, was happening in the past, or will be happening in the future.

*The **present progressive tense** tells about something happening now. It uses the helping verb* is, am, *or* are *and the* –ing *form of the verb.*

Example: The horse **is eating** a carrot.   The skeletons **are walking**.

Change the sentences below from the present tense to the present progressive tense. The first one is done for you.

1. Steve mines for diamonds.

Steve is mining for diamonds.

2. The villagers wait to trade.

_____

3. Alex rides in her minecart.

_____

4. The chicken lays eggs.

_____

5. I play Minecraft with my friends.

_____

PAST PROGRESSIVE TENSE

*The **past progressive tense** tells about something that was happening in the past. It uses the helping verb was or were and the –ing form of the verb. Usually the past progressive tense talks about an action that happened in the middle of another action.*

Example: The zombie **was laughing** when he fell into the lava pit.
The skeletons **were groaning** as they walked.

Change the sentences below from the past tense to the past progressive tense. The first one is done for you.

1. The skeleton ran as it shot its arrows.

The skeleton was running as it shot its arrows.

2. The ghasts threw fireballs as they attacked.

_____

3. Alex smiled as she crafted a golden sword.

_____

4. The creeper plotted revenge while he was in the trap.

_____

5. The torches lit the way as Steve entered the cave.

_____

FUTURE PROGRESSIVE TENSE

*The **future progressive tense** tells about something that will be happening in the future. It uses the helping verb* will be *and the –ing form of the verb. Usually the future progressive tense talks about an action that will be ongoing.*

Example: The horse **will be eating a carrot**.   The skeletons **will be walking**.

Change the sentences below from the present tense to the future progressive tense. The first one is done for you.

1. Alex fights the Ender dragon tomorrow.

Alex will be fighting the Ender dragon tomorrow.

2. The bat flies tonight.

_____

3. I look for some blaze powder to make a potion.

_____

4. The ghast shoots fireballs at the player.

_____

5. Steve crafts a diamond sword next week.

_____

MODAL AUXILIARY VERBS

Modal auxiliary verbs show that something is possible or necessary. Verbs that show something is possible include: can, may, and might. Verbs that show something is necessary include: must and has to/have to.

Underline the modal auxiliary verbs in the sentences below. On the line, write whether the verb shows that something is possible (P) *or* necessary (N). *The first one is done for you.*

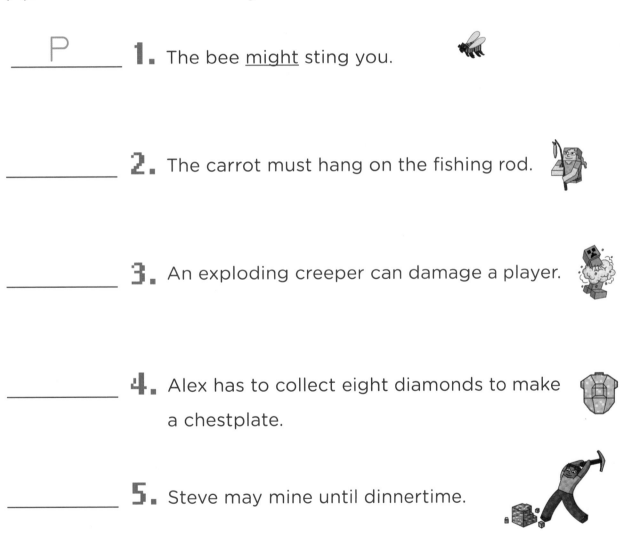

____P____ **1.** The bee <u>might</u> sting you.

_____ **2.** The carrot must hang on the fishing rod.

_____ **3.** An exploding creeper can damage a player.

_____ **4.** Alex has to collect eight diamonds to make a chestplate.

_____ **5.** Steve may mine until dinnertime.

_____ **6.** The witch might brew a potion later.

WRITING A NARRATIVE

Someone hid a very valuable object in a secret room in this witch's hut. Write a story where you walk into the hut. Describe what you discover and what happens next. Use sensory details to describe your experience.

_____

_____

_____

_____

_____

_____

_____

_____

_____

_____

_____

_____

WRITING DIALOGUE

Let's continue the story you started on the previous page. Now imagine that the witch comes home while you are inside the hut. What would you say to her? What would the witch say to you? Write at least five lines of dialogue to describe what happens next. Remember to use quotation marks and commas in the correct places.

SEQUENCE OF EVENTS

*In **expository writing**, ideas, reasons, or steps are presented in a logical order. Words like* first, then, next, after, *and* finally *help show order.*

The bedroom in the picture is very messy. Imagine that this is your bedroom and you have to clean it up. Describe cleaning up the room using the words in the box so the sequence of events makes sense. For example, you can't sweep the floor until you put away all the toys and books on the floor.

first	finally	next
after	then	second

_____

_____

_____

_____

_____

_____

_____

PREFIXES

A **prefix** is a group of letters placed before a word. The prefix changes the meaning of the word into another word. For example, the prefix un- *placed before the word* happy *creates the word* unhappy.

Read the prefixes in the box and their meanings. Combine the prefixes with the words listed to create new words. Some words may have more than one combination.

tele-	**(from afar)**
auto-	**(self)**
photo-	**(light)**

1. phones _____

2. synthesis _____

3. copy _____

4. mobile _____

5. gram _____

6. graph _____

7. biography _____

8. scope _____

MORE PREFIXES

Add one of the prefixes from the box to each line to create a new word with the definition shown. The first one is done for you.

mis- (wrong)	pre- (before)
post- (after)	under- (below)

1. **pre**pare	To get ready in advance
2. _____**understand**	To get something wrong
3. _____**fed**	Malnourished
4. _____**script**	Words or notes after a letter or an article
5. _____**take**	An error
6. _____**arrange**	To arrange in advance
7. _____**age**	Below a certain age
8. _____**dinner**	After dinner

ANTONYMS

An **antonym** is a word opposite in meaning to another word. For example, loud *is an antonym of* quiet. Match the words in the left column with its antonym in the right column.

1. fast

A. dry

2. happy

B. found

3. wet

C. go

4. come

D. wrong

5. lost

E. slow

6. right

F. short

7. tall

G. upset

SYNONYMS

*A **synonym** is a word that's the same in meaning to another word. For example,* loud *is a synonym of* noisy. *Read each row of words and circle the synonyms in each row.*

1. sad   happy   upset   lost

2. slow   fast   quick   run

3. funny   neat   messy   tidy

4. laugh   chuckle   scream   sleep

5. smart   large   small   big

6. dull   boring   exciting   laugh

7. pleasant   large   angry   mad

SENSORY DETAILS

*In writing, **sensory details** describe what a character sees, hears, smells, touches, and tastes. Look at the picture of a diver exploring an underwater shipwreck. Write a paragraph describing the diver's experience using lots of sensory detail.*

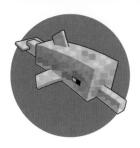

_____

_____

_____

_____

_____

_____

_____

_____

_____

_____

_____

CHARACTER DEVELOPMENT

In writing, character development means the way a character in a story is revealed to the reader. It is always better to reveal a character's traits by what they say and do (showing) rather than describing those traits directly (telling). For example:

(telling)	Alex was annoyed.
(showing)	Alex let out a big sigh and rolled her eyes.

Pick one of the characters in the scene below. Imagine what that person is thinking, saying, and feeling. Then fill out the graphic organizer on the next page.

CHARACTER DEVELOPMENT

Read the instructions on the previous page and fill out the graphic organizer below. Remember, you can make up anything you want!

Name of your character: _____

Three character traits:

1. _____

2. _____

3. _____

What the character says	What the character does
How the character feels	**What the character's body is doing**

CHARACTER DEVELOPMENT

Using your graphic organizer from the previous page, write a short story about your character's day. Remember to show, not tell, the reader what your character is like.

_____

_____

_____

_____

_____

_____

_____

_____

_____

_____

_____

PRESENT PROGRESSIVE TENSE

Present progressive tense is an action that is in progress in the present moment. It uses the helping verb is, am, *or* are and the –ing *form of the verb.*

Example: Alex **is fighting** a dragon.

Read the verbs below. Choose the answer that is in the present progressive tense. The first one is done for you.

1. go

   a. goes   b. is going   c. to go

2. laugh

   a. is laughing   b. laughed   c. will laugh

3. run

   a. ran   b. running   c. am running

4. fight

   a. are fighting   b. fights   c. fought

5. play

   a. plays   b. will play   c. is playing

6. help

   a. will help   b. am helping   c. helps

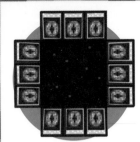

PAST PROGRESSIVE TENSE

The **past progressive tense** tells about something in progress in the past. It uses the helping verb was *or* were *and the* –ing *form of the verb.*

Example: The Enderman **was teleporting** away from me.

Read the verbs below. Choose the answer that is in the past progressive tense. The first one is done for you.

1. closed

    a. was closing   b. was closed   c. will close

2. watched

    a. will be watching   b. is watching   c. were watching

3. talked

    a. talk   b. will talk   c. was talking

4. studied

    a. was studying   b. studying   c. are studying

5. yelled

    a. is yelling   b. were yelling   c. will yell

6. smiled

    a. smiles   b. will smile   c. were smiling

FUTURE PROGRESSIVE TENSE

The **future progressive tense** tells about something in progress in the future. It uses the helping verb will be and the -ing form of the verb.

Example: Steve **will be crafting** a potion tomorrow.

Read the verbs below. Choose the answer that is in the future progressive tense. The first one is done for you.

1. **will speak**

   a. speaks   b. was speaking   c. will be speaking

2. **will act**

   a. will be acting   b. acted   c. were acting

3. **will eat**

   a. eating   b. will be eating   c. is eating

4. **will read**

   a. will be reading   b. was reading   c. reads

5. **will sleep**

   a. sleeps   b. were sleeping   c. will be sleeping

6. **will jump**

   a. will be jumping   b. is jumping   c. jumps

SIMILES

*A **simile** is a figure of speech that directly compares two different things. A simile is usually in a phrase that begins with* as *or* like.

Example: The airplane roared like a lion.
The pillow was as hard as a stone.

*Place an **S** next to the sentences that contain similes. Underline the simile in the sentence. The first one is done for you.*

_____S_____ **1.** The endermite was <u>as quiet as a mouse.</u>

_____ **2.** The lava was hot like the sun.

_____ **3.** The shovel was very sharp.

_____ **4.** The zombies were as green as spring grass.

_____ **5.** Steve slept like a baby.

_____ **6.** The sheep is dyed bright pink.

METAPHORS

A **metaphor** is a figure of speech that is used to make a comparison between two things that aren't alike but do have something in common.

Example: The classroom was a zoo.

Place an **M** next to the sentences that contain metaphors. Underline the metaphor in the sentence. The first one is done for you.

_____M_____ **1.** She is a <u>prickly cactus</u>.

_____ **2.** He was a pig at dinner.

_____ **3.** My brother is a couch potato.

_____ **4.** The ghast was so angry that it screamed.

_____ **5.** That evoker is a real ogre.

_____ **6.** The sun was shining brightly.

SIMILES AND METAPHORS

Now it's your turn. On the lines below, write three similes and three metaphors of your own. Refer back to the previous pages to help you remember which is which.

1. _____

2. _____

3. _____

4. _____

5. _____

MORE PREFIXES

A **prefix** is a group of letters placed before a word. The prefix changes the meaning of the word into another word. Choose the right prefix from the box below to create a new word with the correct meaning. The first one is done for you.

dis-	(not or apart)
re-	(back, again)
mis-	(wrong)

Base Word	Prefix +Base Word	Meaning
1. trust	distrust	**To not trust**
2. model		**To make a model again**
3. understand		**To understand incorrectly**
4. group		**To group again**
5. appear		**To not appear**
6. count		**To not count correctly**

DICTIONARY ENTRY

*A **dictionary entry** does more than define a word. It also tells you how to pronounce the word, what part of speech it is, other forms of the word, how it is used in a sentence, and sometimes synonyms for the word. The entry below is adapted from Merriam-Webster's Dictionary. Read the text and then answer the questions that follow.*

cry | ʻkrī | verb

cried; crying

1. To utter loudly: SHOUT
He *cried* "Wait!" but it was too late.

2. To shed tears often noisily: WEEP, SOB
The child began to *cry* after she dropped her ice-cream cone.

3. To utter a characteristic sound or call
We heard the seagulls *crying*.

DICTIONARY ENTRY

Answer the questions below from the dictionary entry on the previous page.

1. What part of speech is the word *cry*?

_____

2. What are the other forms of the word *cry*?

_____

3. How many definitions are there of the word *cry*?

_____

4. What are some synonyms for the second definition of
the word *cry*?

_____

5. How is the third definition of *cry* used in a sentence?

_____

_____

YOUR DICTIONARY ENTRY

With an adult's help, use a dictionary to find any word you like. Then fill out the form below. You might have to write your own sentences if your dictionary doesn't provide any.

_____ \ _____ \ _____
  (word)   (pronunciation)   (part of speech)

_____
(other forms of the word)

1. _____
   (definition #1)

   _____
   (definition #1 used in a sentence)

2. _____
   (definition #2)

   _____
   (definition #2 used in a sentence)

3. _____
   (definition #3)

   _____
   (definition #3 used in a sentence)

IDIOMS

An **idiom** is a phrase or an expression that means something different from its literal meaning.

Example: It's raining cats and dogs.
Meaning: It's raining a lot.

Match the idiom on the left to it's nonliteral meaning on the right. The first one is done for you.

1. On cloud nine

2. A piece of cake

3. A level playing field

4. Butterflies in my stomach

5. Back to square one

6. Hungry as a bear

7. A drop in the bucket

A. Famished, starving

B. A little bit of what is needed

C. Nervous

D. Very happy, elated

E. Equal, even

F. Starting all over again

G. Very easy

ADAGES

*An **adage** (also called a **proverb**) is an old, short saying that is generally accepted to have some truth to it.*

Example: Beauty is in the eye of the beholder.

Meaning: Everyone has a different idea of what is beautiful.

Match the adage on the top with its meaning below. Write the letter on the line. The first one is done for you.

___B___ **1.** Actions speak louder than words.

_____ **2.** Don't cry over spilled milk.

_____ **3.** The early bird catches the worm.

_____ **4.** The grass is always greener on the other side of the fence.

_____ **5.** Don't put all your eggs in one basket.

_____ **6.** A picture is worth a thousand words.

A. Don't spend your time feeling bad about old mistakes.

B. What you do is more important than what you say.

C. The one who arrives first has the best chance for success.

D. An image conveys meaning better than a description does.

E. People are never satisfied with their own situation; they always think others have it better.

F. Don't put all your hopes on one thing that might not happen.

SUFFIXES

A **suffix** is a group of letters placed at the end of a word. The suffix changes the meaning of the word into another word or into another part of speech. For example, the suffix -less placed at the end of the word fear creates the word fearless.

Read the suffixes in the box and their meanings. Add one of the suffixes to the words in the chart below to create a new word with the correct meaning. The first one is done for you.

-ful	(full of)
-able	(able to be)
-less	(not having)

Base Word	Base Word + Suffix	Meaning
1. worth	worthless	Not valuable
2. comfort		Cozy, pleasant
3. understand		Able to be understood
4. friend		Having no friends
5. wonder		Excellent, terrific
6. hope		Full of optimism

USING TECHNOLOGY

How much do you know about each Minecraft mob? With an adult's help, do some online research to learn more about one Minecraft mob. Use at least two websites. Take notes about what you learn in the space below.

_____

_____

_____

_____

_____

_____

_____

_____

_____

_____

USING TECHNOLOGY

Using the notes you took on the previous page, write four new things you learned about the mob using the categories below.

1. Spawning

_____

2. Behavior

_____

3. Immunity

_____

4. Damage

_____

List the websites you used for your research.

1. _____

2. _____

3. _____

RUN-ON SENTENCES

*A **run-on sentence** occurs when two or more complete sentences are joined without any form of punctuation.*

Example: I love to play Minecraft I would play every day if I had the time.

To correct a run-on sentence, you have two choices:

1. Add a comma and the word and *between the two sentences.*

Example: I love to play Minecraft, and I would play every day if I had the time.

2. Add a period at the end of the first sentence and start the next sentence with a capital letter.

Example: I love to play Minecraft. I would play every day if I had the time.

Correct the run-on sentences below using one of these two methods.

1. The creeper has block-shaped feet it is green.

_____

2. Steve likes to tame wolves to keep as pets he puts red

collars on them.

_____

3. Alex fought the wither with all her strength her bow and

arrow came in very handy.

_____

4. The player was very sneaky he stole everything out of my chest.

_____

5. Alex uses a pickaxe to mine for diamonds she will make a diamond sword when she is done.

_____

6. Steve made eye contact with the Enderman the Enderman teleported toward him.

_____

7. Diamond swords are very useful they can destroy blazes, Endermen, and zombies.

_____

8. Building a house in Minecraft is fun you must add doors to keep out hostile mobs.

_____

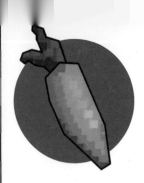

SEQUENCE OF EVENTS

Use the transition words in the box and the numbered pictures to tell the story of how Alex rode a pig. Don't forget to write a conclusion.

first	then	next	after	finally

1.

2.

3.

4.

5.

6.

QUOTATION MARKS

An ender dragon has destroyed all the quotation marks and commas in the sentences below. Add the missing quotation marks and commas in the correct places to win an ender pearl. The first one has been done for you.

1. "The enderman dropped an ender pearl," said Steve.

2. I need to kill a blaze said Alex so I can get a blaze rod.

3. Steve said Quick! Toss the blaze rod on the crafting table.

4. Cool said Alex. Now we have blaze powder.

5. If we craft the ender pearl and blaze rod together, we'll get an eye of ender explained Steve.

6. Alex said Let's throw the eye of ender to find the nearest end portal.

7. There it is said Steve. Let's go!

REMEMBERING DETAILS

Below is a picture of a farm in Minecraft. Study the picture for a minute or two. When you think you have memorized the details, try to answer the questions on the back of the page without looking!

REMEMBERING DETAILS

(continued from previous page)

Answer the questions in the space provided.

1. How many chickens are in the picture?

_____

2. What are the two largest animals in the picture?

_____

3. What three colors are on the barn?

_____

4. Where is the cat in the picture?

_____

5. What is behind the barn?

_____

6. What color is the sky?

_____

CAPITALIZATION

Capital letters are used at the beginning of a sentence, at the beginning of a quote, for the word "I," and for proper nouns such as names and places. The wither has used its wither skulls to destroy all the capital letters in the sentences below. Use a marker to add the capital letters back in so you can fight the wither and win the game. The first one is done for you.

1. "We need to craft some diamond armor to defeat Mr. Wither," said Alex.

2. "good idea," replied steve. "i also have a diamond sword that i got in ender city."

3. alex was busy looking for soul sand in minetown. she knew she had to arrange them in the shape of a t.

4. "look! it's three wither skulls," said steve. "we got lucky. these are hard to find."

5. the two friends backed away as the wither regained his health."

6. steve whispered to alex, "don't attack yet. he will explode soon."

7. "now!" alex yelled. "watch out for the flying skulls!"

CERTIFICATE OF ACHIEVEMENT
CONGRATULATIONS

This certifies that

_____

became a

MINECRAFT WRITING BOSS

on _____.
(date)

_____

Signature

ANSWER KEY

PAGE 2
Sensory Detail
Answers will vary.

PAGE 3
Adjective Order
1. The villager wore a long, white robe.
2. I am building a big, gray, cobblestone shelter.
3. A single, rare, golden apple cured the zombie villager.
4. Watch out for the dangerous, black Ender dragon!
5. The Nether is full of many valuable resources.

PAGES 4–5
Sentences
1. The scary wither angrily attacks a player.
2. A dizzy zombie groans loudly.
3. A skeleton secretly fires poison arrows.
4. Quickly hide your loot in a large chest.
5. Never approach an exploding creeper.

PAGE 6
Redstone Research
Answers will vary but may include:
1. Redstone can be used to craft compasses, clocks, and powered rails.
2. Redstone can be used to craft other redstone blocks.
3. Redstone can be used to craft redstone lamps, note blocks, detector rails, and redstone torches.
4. Redstone will power dust and repeaters.
5. Redstone can be used to deactivate attached torches and activate mechanisms.

PAGE 7
Headings for Heroes
Answers will vary but should be something like the following:
1. The Types of Weapons in Minecraft
2. The Beginning of Minecraft

PAGE 8
Quotation Marks
Alex was getting tired of fighting Creeper. She put down her sword. "Steve is having a party," she said. "Want to come?"

Creeper looked confused. "What is a party?" he asked.

"It's a lot of fun. Come and I'll show you."

When they arrived at Steve's house, Creeper saw kids running in the backyard and streamers and balloons hanging) from the ceiling. A table was piled with presents, cupcakes, and party hats.

"Hi, Alex. Thanks for coming to my party," Steve said.

"Happy birthday, Steve," Alex replied. "This is Creeper."

Creeper looked frightened. Steve handed him a piece of cake on a plate with a fork. Creeper didn't know what the fork was for, so he used his feet to eat. "It's delicious," he said with his mouth full.

PAGE 9

Fact vs. Opinion

_____O_____ 1. Minecraft is a very hard game to play.

_____O_____ 2. Minecraft is best played in Creative Mode.

_____F_____ 3. Exploding creepers can damage a player.

_____F_____ 4. Pigs can be tamed with a carrot.

_____O_____ 5. The Enderman is the scariest of all the mobs.

_____F_____ 6. You need 24 blocks of diamonds to make a full suit of armor.

PAGE 10—11

Plan Your Writing
Answers will vary.

Write Your Opinion
Answers will vary.

PAGES 12—13

Commonly Confused Words

1. their
2. there
3. their
4. they're
5. its
6. It's
7. it's
8. two
9. too
10. to
11. two, to
12. loose
13. lose

PAGE 14

Write about a Topic
Answers will vary.

PAGE 15

Linking Ideas in Your Writing
Answers will vary.

PAGE 16

Relative Pronouns

Minecraft is the video game (that) most kids play.

Minecraft, (which) can be played in Survival Mode or Creative Mode, is exciting.

Pigs are animals (that) can be tamed with a carrot.

Is (that) the mob that chased you?

The Enderman (that) finishes first wins the race.

The player (who) built the snow golem is very clever.

That's the chest (which) holds her armor.

That's the player (whose) armor is gold.

PAGE 17

More Relative Pronouns

1. Alex is the girl ___who___ is hugging the pig.

2. The diamond ___that___ Alex is holding is shiny.

3. The diamond sword ___that___ Steve made is very sharp.

4. The witch ___whose___ potion I used is wearing a purple robe.

5. The villager ___who___ grew the glistening melon is a good farmer.

PAGE 18

Present Progressive Tense

1. Steve is mining for diamonds.
2. The villagers are waiting to trade.
3. Alex is riding in her minecart.
4. The chicken is laying eggs.
5. I am playing Minecraft with my friends.

PAGE 19
Past Progressive Tense

1. <u>The skeleton was running as it shot its arrows.</u>

2. The ghasts were throwing fireballs as they attacked.

3. Alex was smiling as she crafted a golden sword.

4. The creeper was plotting revenge while he was in the trap.

5. The torches were lighting the way as Steve entered the cave.

PAGE 20
Future Progressive Tense

1. <u>Alex will be fighting the Ender dragon tomorrow.</u>

2. The bat will be flying tonight.

3. I will be looking for some blaze powder to make a potion.

4. The ghast will be shooting fireballs at the player.

5. Steve will be crafting a diamond sword next week.

PAGE 21
Modal Auxiliary Verbs

_____P_____ 1. The bee might sting you.

_____N_____ 2. The carrot must hang on the fishing rod.

_____P_____ 3. An exploding creeper can damage a player.

_____N_____ 4. Alex has to collect eight diamonds to make a chestplate.

_____P_____ 5. Steve may mine until dinnertime.

_____P_____ 6. The witch might brew a potion later.

PAGE 22
Writing a Narrative

Answers will vary but should include a narrator, a sequence of events, and sensory details.

PAGE 23
Writing Dialogue

Answers will vary but should include at least five lines of dialogue and correct placement of commas and quotation marks.

PAGE 24
Sequence of Events

Answers will vary.

PAGE 25
Prefixes

1. telephone
2. photosynthesis
3. photocopy
4. automobile
5. telegram
6. telegraph, autograph, photograph
7. autobiography
8. telescope

PAGE 26
More Prefixes

prepare

misunderstand

underfed

postscript

mistake

prearrange

underage

postdinner

PAGE 27
Antonyms

Fast — Slow
Happy — Upset
Wet — Dry
Come — Go
Lost — Found
Right — Wrong
Tall — Short

PAGE 28
Synonyms

(sad) happy (upset) lost

slow (fast) (quick) run

funny (neat) messy (tidy)

(laugh) (chuckle) scream sleep

smart (large) small (big)

(dull) (boring) exciting laugh

pleasant large (angry) (mad)

PAGE 29
Sensory Details

Answers will vary but should include the what the diver sees, hears, smells, touches, and tastes.

PAGES 30–32
Character Development

Answers will vary but should include details about what the character is feeling, doing, and saying.

PAGE 33
Present Progressive Tense

1b, 2a, 3c, 4a, 5c, 6b

PAGE 34
Past Progressive Tense

1a, 2c, 3c, 4a, 5b, 6c

PAGE 35
Future Progressive Tense

1c, 2a, 3b, 4a, 5c, 6a

PAGE 36
Similes

__S__ 1. The endermite was as <u>quiet as a mouse.</u>
__S__ 2. The lava was <u>hot like the sun.</u>
_____ 3. The shovel was very sharp.
__S__ 4. The zombies were as <u>green as spring grass.</u>
__S__ 5. Steve slept <u>like a baby.</u>
_____ 6. The sheep is dyed bright pink.

PAGE 37
Metaphors

__M__ 1. She is a prickly cactus.
__M__ 2. He was a pig at dinner.
__M__ 3. My brother is a couch potato.
_____ 4. The ghast was so angry that it screamed.
__M__ 5. That evoker is a real ogre.
_____ 6. The sun was shining brightly.

PAGE 38
Similes and Metaphors

Answers will vary.

PAGE 39
More Prefixes

Base Word	Prefix +Base Word	Meaning
trust	distrust	To not trust
model	remodel	To make a model again
understand	misunderstand	To understand incorrectly
group	regroup	To group again
prove	disappear	To not appear
count	miscount	To count incorrectly

PAGES 40—41
Dictionary Entry
1. verb
2. cried, crying
3. three
4. weep, sob
5. We heard the seagulls crying.

PAGE 42
Your Dictionary Entry
Answers will vary.

PAGE 43
Idioms

1. On cloud nine
2. A piece of cake
3. A level playing field
4. Butterflies in my stomach
5. Back to square one
6. Hungry as a bear
7. A drop in the bucket

A. Famished, starving
B. A little bit of what is needed
C. Nervous
D. Very happy, elated
E. Equal, even
F. Starting all over again
G. Very easy

PAGE 44
Adages

___B___ 1. Actions speak louder than words.

___A___ 2. Don't cry of spilled milk.

___C___ 3. The early bird catches the worm.

___E___ 4. The grass is always greener on the other side of the fence.

___F___ 6. Don't put all your eggs in one basket.

___D___ 7. A picture is worth a thousand words.

PAGE 45
Suffixes

Base Word	Base Word + Suffix	Meaning
worth	worthless	Not valuable
comfort	comfortable	Cozy, pleasant
understand	understandable	Able to be understood
friend	friendless	Having no friends
wonder	wonderful	Excellent, terrific
hope	hopeful	Full of optimism

PAGE 46—47
Using Technology
Answers will vary.

PAGE 48—49
Run-On Sentences
1. *The creeper has block-shaped feet, and it is green.*
OR
The creeper has block-shaped feet. It is green.

2. *Steve likes to tame wolves to keep as pets, and he puts red collars on them.*
OR
Steve likes to tame wolves to keep as pets. He puts red collars on them.

3. *Alex fought the wither with all her strength, and her bow and arrow came in very handy.*
OR
Alex fought the wither with all her strength. Her bow and arrow came in very handy.

4. *The player was very sneaky, and he stole everything out of my chest.*
OR
The player was very sneaky. He stole everything out of my chest.

5. *Alex uses a pickaxe to mine for diamonds, and she will make a diamond sword when she is done.*

OR

Alex uses a pickaxe to mine for diamonds. She will make a diamond sword when she is done.

6. *Steve made eye contact with the Enderman, and the Enderman teleported toward him.*

OR

Steve made eye contact with the Enderman. The Enderman teleported toward Steve.

7. *Diamond swords are very useful, and they can destroy blazes, Endermen, and zombies.*

OR

Diamond swords are very useful. They can destroy blazes, Endermen, and zombies.

8. *Building a house in Minecraft is fun, and you must to add doors to keep out hostile mobs.*

OR

Building a house in Minecraft is fun. You must add doors to keep out hostile mobs.

PAGES 50—51
Sequence of Events

Wording will vary but should include the following details:

First, Alex was patting her pig. Then Alex started thinking about how she could tame her pig. Then Alex had an idea and she ran to get a carrot. Next, Alex put the carrot on the fishing rod. After, she put the saddle on the pig. Finally, she got on the saddle and held the carrot above the pig's head. It worked!

PAGE 52
Quotation Marks

1. "The enderman dropped an ender pearl," said Steve.

2. "I need to kill a blaze," said Alex, "so I can get a blaze rod."

3. Steve said, "Quick! Toss the blaze rod on the crafting table."

4. "Cool," said Alex. "Now we have blaze powder."

5. "If we craft the ender pearl and blaze rod together, we'll get an eye of ender," explained Steve.

6. Alex said, "Let's throw the eye of ender to find the nearest end portal."

7. "There it is," said Steve. "Let's go!"

PAGES 53—54
Remembering Details

1. two
2. the pig and the horse
3. red, white, and brown
4. sitting on the fence
5. trees, mountains, clouds
6. blue

PAGE 55
Capitalization

1. "We need to craft some diamond armor to defeat Mr. Wither," said Alex.

2. "Good idea," replied Steve. "I also have a diamond sword that I found in Ender City."

3. Alex was busy looking for soul sand in Minetown. She knew she had to arrange them in the shape of a T.

4. "Look! It's three wither skulls," said Steve. "We got lucky. These are hard to find."

5. The two friends backed away as the wither regained his health.

6. Steve whispered to Alex, "Don't attack yet. He will explode soon."

7. "Now!" Alex yelled. "Watch out for the flying skulls!"